Fiddle Primer Deluxe Edition

by Jim Tolles

This course includes both physical Book/DVD/CDs and Free Digital Video & Audio Access

+

Free Digital Access

For computer or mobile device

To receive free digital video & audio access, send an email to:
fiddle@cvls.com

Copyright 2016 by Watch & Learn, Inc. Second Edition
ALL RIGHTS RESERVED. Any copying, arranging, or adapting of this work without the consent of the owner is an infringement of copyright.

HOW TO USE THE

If you are using the *Fiddle Primer* book and DVD together, follow these suggestions.

Step 1
Watch a section of the DVD. Rewind and watch again until you understand it completely. (A section would be from one title page to the next).

Step 2
Once you understand the section, go to the book to practice the exercises and songs over and over until you are comfortable with them.

Step 3
After practicing with the book, go back to the DVD and play along to make sure you are performing the material properly.

This course is designed to be worked through, stopping and practicing each section until you are thoroughly familiar with it. It will probably take the average beginning student 2 - 4 months to work all the way through the book and DVD, so don't get in a hurry. Take your time and learn the material correctly.

DEDICATION

This book is dedicated to my students. All have helped me grow as a teacher, just as I hope I have helped them grow as fiddlers.

INTRODUCTION

The *Fiddle Primer Deluxe Edition* with DVD and audio CD will quickly transform you from an absolute beginner into a student/fiddler with a full understanding of the fundamentals and techniques of playing the fiddle. This clear, step-by-step method includes many photographs, large easy to read notation, and a sequence of learning that has been meticulously developed and tested over a 30 year period. With each new song, you will learn new techniques to establish a firm foundation that will enable you to enjoy playing fiddle for many years. The companion DVD provides the accent, tone, and rhythm for all the songs and exercises in this book and you will progress even faster because you will be able to see the correct movements of the left and right hand. It's no wonder the *Fiddle Primer* is the first choice of over 2,000 stores throughout the United States and Canada.

THE AUTHOR

Jim Tolles has been playing violin and fiddle for 30 years and teaching for 25. He is an accomplished performer, having appeared with Goose Creek Symphony, Breakfast Special, touring Broadway shows, and numerous country and bluegrass bands native to his Atlanta, Georgia home. He is currently a full time teacher in Atlanta. Jim has recorded with various artists on the Capitol, Atteiram, and Rounder labels and has written songs on those labels as well as Flying Fish. Jim's playing has been featured on national radio and TV commercials. This course is a product of those 25 years of teaching and his desire to help the beginning player get off to the best possible start. Jim also wrote *The Violin Primer* book and *Introduction to Violin* DVD.

WATCH & LEARN PRODUCTS REALLY WORK

25 years ago, Watch & Learn revolutionized music instructional courses by developing well thought out, step-by-step instructional methods combined with clear, easy-to-understand graphics that were tested for effectiveness on beginners before publication. This concept, which has dramatically improved the understanding and success of beginning students, has evolved into the Watch & Learn mastermind of authors, editors, teachers, and artists that continue to set the standard of music instruction today. This has resulted in sales of almost 1.5 million products since 1979. This high quality course will significantly increase your success and enjoyment while playing the fiddle.

CD & DVD COUNTER

The CD & DVD counters are included in the *Fiddle Primer* book to show you where each lesson is located on the companion CD or DVD. Use your remote control on the CD or DVD player to skip to the track you want.

TABLE OF CONTENTS

SECTION I - Getting Started	Book	CD 1	DVD 2-3
Parts of the Fiddle & Bow	1	01	2-3
Shoulder Rest	2		
Bow Preparation	3		4
Tuning	4	02	5
Holding The Fiddle	5		6
Left Hand Position	8		7
Left Arm Position	9		
Holding The Bow	10		8
Bowing Open Strings	12		9
Music Notation	14		16
Open String Exercises	15	03-11	10-15
Noting The Fiddle	20	12-17	17-22
Our First Song	22	18	23
Here We Go	23	19	24
Mary Had A Little Lamb	24	20-23	25-28
G, A, & B Notes	26	24-27	29-32
The Alphabet Song	27	28-29	33-35
Practice	28		36

SECTION II - PLAYING

	Book	CD 1	DVD 2-3
Slurs	30	30-34	37-41
Go Tell Aunt Rhody	32	35	42-45
The D Scale	34	39-49	46-52
3/4 Time	37	50	53-56
Sunday Waltz	38	51	57-58

SECTION III - FIDDLE TUNES

Title	Book	CD 1
You Are My Sunshine	41	52-53
E & F# Notes	42	54-55
Wildwood Flower	43	56-57
Eighth Notes	44	58-59
Hot Corn Cold Corn	45	60-61
Amazing Grace	46	62-63
Dotted Rhythms	47	64-65
Blind Mary	48	66
C Natural	49	67
Star of the County Down	50	68-70
Southwind	52	71-72
Will The Circle Be Unbroken	53	73-75
The A Note	54	76-78
Angeline The Baker	55	79-80
Little Maggie	56	81-82
Double Stops	57	83
Shuffle	58	84
Boil Them Cabbage Down	59	85
Soldier's Joy	60	86-87
Cripple Creek	61	88-89
Red Haired Boy	62	90-91
Salt Creek	63	92-93
Roll In My Sweet Baby's Arms	64	94-95
Old Joe Clark	65	96

SECTION 1
GETTING STARTED

PARTS OF THE FIDDLE AND BOW

Wooden Friction Pegs
Scroll
Nut
Fingerboard
Strings
Purfling
Bridge
F hole
Fine Tuners
Tailpiece
Chin Rest
Tail Pin
Button or Screw

Tip
Hair
Stick →
Frog

Take your fiddle and bow to your local music store to make sure they are in proper working order. See that the strings are in good condition and that the bow has enough hair and works properly. Also have them tune it for you.

If you are teaching yourself to play the fiddle without the aid of a teacher, we feel that using both the DVD and the book will make learning much easier. There are many details to holding the fiddle and bow, and using both teaching methods will enable you to learn proper techniques much faster.

SHOULDER REST

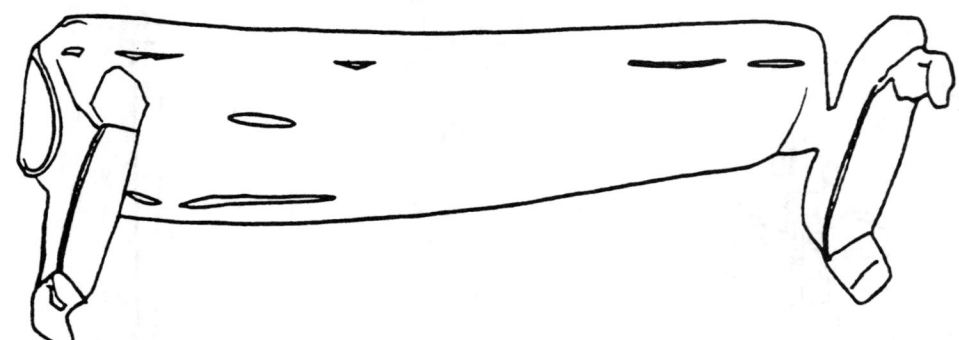

Get a shoulder rest that looks like this. There are several different kinds on the market and you may need to experiment, but we recommend this one.

FINE TUNERS

Fine tuner

Have fine tuners installed on the tailpiece. These are a necessity if you have steel strings on your fiddle. If you are playing on nylon strings, only one fine tuner is required for the E string or 1st string.

BOW PREPARATION

TIGHTENING & LOOSENING

Before playing, tighten the bow. Turn the screw clockwise so that the bow hair comes away from the stick, but not so much that you lose the curve of the bow. When you're finished playing, loosen the bow so that when you tap the stick, the bow hair just begins to flop.

ROSIN

Fiddlers play with different amounts of rosin. First, tighten the bow in order to apply rosin. Draw the bow back and forth against the rosin. Press hard and use short strokes. When you feel you have enough, use long strokes to distribute the rosin. If the bow just barely makes a sound on the strings, you need more rosin. If clouds of rosin come flying off as you play, you have too much rosin.

REHAIRING

Bow hairs do break and eventually you will need to have your bow rehaired. Have your bow checked to make sure it does not need to be rehaired.

← Button or Screw

TUNING THE FIDDLE

You should tune the fiddle at the start of every practice session. The wooden friction pegs are used to make large changes in pitch (see page 1). The fine tuners make smaller changes. Bow the D or 3rd string. If it is a long way out of tune, pluck it and turn the friction peg. Then bow the string and simultaneously turn the fine tuner by reaching underneath the fiddle. At first you may need to take your fiddle to a music store or fiddle teacher for help.

AUDIO CD OR DVD

Listen to the CD or DVD to hear the correct pitch. Tune close to the correct pitch with the wooden friction pegs, then use the fine tuners to make it exact. Tune all four strings in this manner.

PIANO

If you have a piano or keyboard at home, it can be used as a tuning source. The following diagram shows which note on the piano matches each open string of the fiddle.

ELECTRONIC TUNER

I recommend that you purchase an electronic tuner as soon as possible. They cost about $30 - $50 at your local music store and will enable you to tune very easily. Most stores will be happy to show you how to use the tuner.

HOLDING THE FIDDLE

You can play the fiddle standing or sitting. Standing helps many folks get the feel of the instrument and avoids the problem of the bow hitting your leg while seated. We recommend that beginners practice standing up. Check the following diagrams.

Sitting

Standing

HOLDING THE FIDDLE

Put the fiddle under your chin and over your left collarbone. You should be able to support the fiddle without using your left hand. The chin rest is really a jaw bone rest. Turn your head so that it is halfway between straight ahead and looking down the fiddle.

The fiddle should be at a thirty degree angle to the left arm.

The fiddle should be parallel to the floor, not tilted up or down.

6

HOLDING THE FIDDLE

The fiddle should have an easy slope towards the floor. The following diagram shows the correct angle.

Stand in front of a mirror to compare yourself to the above diagram.

LEFT HAND POSITION

Next we'll check your left hand to make sure you are holding the neck of the fiddle properly. Take the V that your thumb and forefinger make (Figure A) and close it so that the neck of the fiddle makes contact with your thumb, just above the first joint, and the side of your hand on that bump where your forefinger joins on (Figure B).

This will create a small space below the neck. Don't let the neck of the fiddle fall into this space. Figure C shows the fiddle from the player's perspective.

Figure A

Contact Points

Figure B

Figure C

LEFT ARM POSITION

The left elbow should be under the fiddle, as far as it will go, not out to the side as illustrated in the following diagrams.

Correct   **Incorrect**

The wrist should be straight or bent slightly away from you. Do not let the wrist collapse or touch the rib of the instrument.

Correct   **Incorrect**

HOLDING THE BOW

Put the fiddle down so that you have both hands free to learn how to hold the bow. We will follow four steps:

1. Form a backwards C with the thumb and middle fingers of the right hand, bending the joint of the thumb as closely as possible to a right angle.

2. Now press the tip of your thumb into the middle joint of your middle and ring fingers. These are the primary points of contact.

3. Holding the bow with your left hand, grasp the bow near the frog on the thumb leather. The index finger goes on at the first joint about 3/4 of an inch up the bow. The pinky is arched and touches at the tip. The thumb touches the bow hair.

HOLDING THE BOW

4. At this point you may notice that your fingers are at right angles to the stick. Turn them so that they are at about a 45 degree angle. Now hold your hand in front of a mirror and compare it to the following diagrams (remember the thumb is still at a right angle).

Points of contact on right hand

This bow grip may seem awkward so allow some time for the muscles in your hand to strengthen and stretch.

Pick up the fiddle and put it under your chin. The bow must be at right angles to the strings at all times. It can be difficult to look down at the bow and strings and tell just when you have a right angle.

An easy solution is to stand in front of a mirror. Turn your body so that the neck of the fiddle is parallel to the mirror. Then turn your head in the chin rest and look in the mirror and it will be possible to make small corrections quite easily.

BOWING OPEN STRINGS

It is very important to be able to bow open strings correctly before trying to play melodies on the fiddle. An open string means one that is not being pressed down by a finger of the left hand.

The bow should strike the strings halfway between the bridge and the end of the fingerboard. The bow should travel across the strings at a right angle, not slanted in either direction.

The action of the arm, if held stiffly, will cause the bow to move awkwardly, so use the shoulder, elbow, and wrist to make it go straight. Use plenty of fluid wrist action. When your right hand approaches the strings, your wrist should be bent upward. As it moves away, the wrist should bend downward as follows:

Wrist Up
Near the strings

Wrist Down
Away from the strings

BOWING OPEN STRINGS

The right elbow should be no higher than the bow. This will vary, depending on which string you are bowing.

Correct

Incorrect

MUSIC NOTATION

As we begin to bow the strings, we'll gradually explain how to read music. The five horizontal lines are called the staff (see diagram below). At the extreme left of music written for fiddle, you will see the treble clef. Notes may be written on the lines or in spaces in between the lines. Higher pitches are written on physically higher positions on the staff, lower notes on lower positions. The notes of our common major scale alternate space, line, space, line, etc. The pitch sounded by bowing the open 3rd string is D. Its location is in the space below the bottom line of the staff. This will be the 1st note of our scale. The next note in the scale is E, found on the bottom line.

We'll introduce rhythm or meter right here. Reading left to right, the staff has bar lines every so often. The spaces between these lines are called bars or measures. Within each measure there is always the same number of pulses or beats. The time signature at the left tells us how many beats per measure. In the example here, we'll use 4/4 time. The top number tells us how many beats per measure. The bottom number tells us what kind of note receives 1 beat. In this case, the 4 on the bottom indicates a quarter note. A quarter note has a solid head and a stem and receives 1 beat. We'll also need to know half notes. They have open heads and stems and receive 2 beats. After playing all of the exercises in the following section along with the CD or DVD, you should have a clear understanding of musical notation.

EXERCISE 1

Now we are ready to start bowing open strings. First check your bow grip. Next, place the hair of the bow on the 3rd string near the frog. Draw the bow out to the tip to a count of 4 (this is a down bow). Draw the bow back to the frog to a count of 4 (this is an up bow). There should be as little break in sound as possible between the down bow and the up bow. Try not to let the bow slow down at the end of the stroke and connect one note to another. Play along with the CD or DVD.

⊓ = down bow
V = up bow

Compare yourself to the DVD or practice in front of a mirror to make sure that you are using the proper technique.

EXERCISE 2

As we go from string to string, we must change the bow angle. The angle of the bow is critical to avoid hitting adjacent strings. Drop the angle of the bow down to play the 2nd string. Then play the same 4 count exercise on the 2nd string.

EXERCISE 3

Drop the angle of the bow even further for the 1st string.

EXERCISE 4

Bring the bow all the way back up for the 4th string.

HALF NOTES

EXERCISE 5

Next we'll bow down and up to the count of 2, playing half notes. Put the bow on the 3rd string (D string) just below the middle. Draw it out to within a few inches of the tip and back to where you started. Count 1, 2 for the down bow and 3, 4 for the up bow. Play along with the CD or DVD.

EXERCISE 6

Now for half notes on the 2nd string or A string.

EXERCISE 7

Again, the same thing on the first string or E string.

EXERCISE 8

Now back down to the 4th string or G string.

QUARTER NOTES

EXERCISE 8A

Now for short bow strokes. Place the bow on the 3rd string (D string), just above the middle, draw it out about 5 or 6 inches and back again without stopping, one count for each bow stroke. These are called quarter notes.

— Quarter note

EXERCISE 9

Now, the same technique on the 2nd string (A string).

EXERCISE 10

To the first string (E string).

EXERCISE 11

Now the 4th string (G string).

There are two primary factors that contribute to good tone and bowing on the fiddle: bow speed and bow pressure. Practice varying these two factors to get a pleasing tone. Too slow with too much pressure produces the horrible grinding sound. Too fast makes a breathy indistinct sound. Too close to the bridge makes a whistling sound.

OPEN STRING EXERCISES

In the following exercises, we will use quarter notes, half notes, and whole notes and swap back and forth from the D string (3rd string) to the A string (2nd string). Play along with the CD to make sure you are playing each exercise correctly.

EXERCISE 12

EXERCISE 13

EXERCISE 14

EXERCISE 15

18

EXERCISE 16

 EXERCISE 17

Play all of these exercises several times until you are comfortable with all of them. Make sure you play along with the CD.

NOTING THE FIDDLE

Now we'll start using the left hand to press down the strings in order to play different notes. Review the left hand and wrist positions we covered earlier.

EXERCISE 19

With your index finger (first finger), press down on the 3rd string about 1 1/8 inches from the nut. Place the bow on the 3rd string a little closer to the frog than the middle. Bow down on the open D string, then up, noting E with your index finger. What you are doing is playing the 1st & 2nd notes of a D major scale. Bow down and up, making small adjustments until you can match this pitch, neither too high or too low. Listen to the CD or DVD.

EXERCISE 20

Below you will see two measures that we will repeat many times. First D, played for a half note, 2 beats, on the down bow, then E, a half note, on the up bow for a total of 2 beats. I'll play the 1st measure and you play the 2nd measure. We'll call these answer backs. Play along with the CD or DVD.

The goal of this exercise is to learn just where that note is, both with your ears and it's location on the fingerboard. Rewind the CD or DVD and answer back many times. Make sure you are in tune and match the pitch exactly. It will take some practice.

EXERCISE 21

Next we'll learn the F# note. It's noted with the 2nd finger, about another inch or so up the fingerboard from the 1st finger. What we are doing is constructing the distance from the 1st note to the 3rd note of a major scale. Its location on the staff is in the bottom space. We'll put the sharp in the key signature on the left hand side of the staff, indicating that all F's, including the one in the bottom space, are sharp.

If your F# is too high (sharp) or too low (flat), don't stop the bow. Continue to play smoothly and make a correction, up or down, on the next answer back.

 ## EXERCISE 22

Now we'll do another set of answer backs that should make it even easier to find these notes. This exercise will include A, the open 2nd string, located on the staff in the next to bottom space. Bow the open D, then E with your index finger, then the open A, then back to the E with your index finger. This will give you 2 points of reference for pitch, the D & A strings, and two opportunities to make those little corrections. Check your bow grip and we're off.

 ## EXERCISE 23

Now the same with the 2nd finger on F#. First open D, then F#, open A (the second string), and back to F#.

This section of the book could well prove invaluable to you as your ear improves. What may have sounded in tune the first few days might seem questionable as your ear gets a better idea of just where these notes are. This is all a normal part of improvement.

 ## EXERCISE 24

Let's walk up the fingerboard using our 3 notes, D, E, & F#. Open D, 1st finger, 2nd finger.

← Teacher →   ← Student →

 # OUR FIRST SONG

We're just about ready to play a tune. First we'll divide the song into exercises before we try to put it all together. Play along with the CD or DVD.

EXERCISE 25

EXERCISE 26

EXERCISE 27

Playing small parts, especially the difficult or unfamiliar parts, helps insure success when you finally dive in to play the whole piece.

HERE WE GO

You should practice this song over and over, playing along with the CD or DVD until you feel comfortable with it and can play it correctly.

MARY HAD A LITTLE LAMB

Frequently it helps beginners to play pieces they know, songs they hear in their head, or can sing. Our next piece is *Mary Had A Little Lamb*, a song virtually everyone is familiar with. Again, we will divide it into exercises.

EXERCISE 28

EXERCISE 29

EXERCISE 30

EXERCISE 31

Now for the complete song.

MARY HAD A LITTLE LAMB

EXERCISE 32

Practice the following exercises, playing along with the CD.

EXERCISE 33

EXERCISE 34

We're ready to learn three new notes: G, A, & B. The first is G. It's located on the next to bottom line, and it is noted with the third finger (ring finger), but instead of being another inch or so up the fingerboard, it is right next to the second finger. On most people's hands, the 2nd & 3rd fingers will touch or very nearly touch. Let's walk up to this note using the notes we already know: D, E, F#, and then G.

EXERCISE 35

EXERCISE 36

Let's add the open A string to our row of notes, D, E, F#, & G to play the first five notes of a major scale, both up and down.

EXERCISE 37

We have five notes in a row and now here comes the sixth. It's B, the note played with the first finger on the A string (or the 2nd string). It's as far up the A string as the E was up the D string. It's location on the staff is on the middle line. Let's do some answer backs, A to B in half notes.

26

At this point we have enough notes to play the *Alphabet Song*. Let's divide it up into exercises.

EXERCISE 38

EXERCISE 39

EXERCISE 40

Now we'll put the whole song together.

 # THE ALPHABET SONG

PRACTICE

The most important part of learning to play the fiddle is to develop consistent and efficient practice habits. The beginning student must have patience because playing the fiddle requires training the hands to do movements they have never done before and to strengthen muscles not normally used. You should average 30 minutes of practice each day. With consistent practice, you should be comfortable with the fiddle and be able to play a few songs slowly within 4 - 6 weeks. Once you learn to play a few things on the fiddle, you'll find the learning process comes easier and your progress will start to snowball.

The following are some helpful hints and pointers concerning practice:

1. Go over your lesson assignment EVERY day. On days that it seems impossible to practice, make yourself go over the lesson for 4 or 5 minutes to reinforce things.
2. Practice 30 minutes a day if you are a beginner and divide this time into 10 or 15 minute segments. It has been proven that the human mind cannot concentrate heavily for more than 15 minutes.
3. Set up practice times to coincide with other activities such as when you wake up, when you go to bed, or when you come home at the end of the day. 15 minutes in the morning and 15 minutes at night works well for many people.
4. If possible set up a special practice area. Buy an inexpensive music stand and keep your lessons on it so you can start to work immediately with each practice session.
5. Avoid marathon 2 or 3 hour practice sessions on the weekends. The mind can only concentrate for short periods and most marathon sessions accomplish about the same amount of learning as a 15 minute practice session. In addition, many students use the "Marathon Practice Session" as an excuse to not practice every day.
6. Learn to identify and focus on the hard parts of each song. Put your efforts there as opposed to playing a song from start to finish over and over. Some techniques and movements require several hundred repetitions over several weeks while others are learned immediately after a few tries.
7. Practice the fiddle at first by looking in a mirror to make sure you are using the proper position.
8. Relax - if frustrated with a particular measure or technique, go to another or just take a break and come back after you feel better.
9. Ask your teacher or a friend to let you know how you are doing every couple of weeks. It is very encouraging because they notice your progress even though you think you are standing still. It's the same thing that happened when you were little and hadn't seen your cousins for a couple of years and were amazed by how much they had grown. They did not notice the growth because it was so gradual on a daily basis.
10. Record and listen to your own playing. This will help you locate areas that need work and also measure progress. Your tapes will improve as you practice more and more.
11. Remember always - Fiddle playing is a lot of fun no matter what your level of competence. Relax and enjoy yourself.

SECTION II
SONGS

SLURS

For out next song, we're gong to learn a new bowing technique. It's called slurring or playing two or more notes on a bow stroke.

EXERCISE 43

Draw a down bow on the 3rd string (D string) for one beat of D, then finger the E note with the index finger for one beat, all without stopping the bow. Continue with the up bow on open D for the 3rd beat, and finger the E with the index finger on the 4th beat. Here's what it looks like written out.

Slur

The curved line connecting the D to the E is the slur. In fiddle music, it means to play all the notes connected by that bow on either one up bow or one down bow. Let's get started on this with just two notes per bow and we'll do it in the form of answer backs. I'll play four beats, you play four beats.

It'll probably feel a little awkward, like patting your head and rubbing your stomach, because you're used to changing notes with the left hand as you change bow directions. Just practice slowly until you get more comfortable with it.

EXERCISE 44

There are other possibilities with slurring and we'll do them all in answer backs. First, notes going down, in this case, F# to E.

EXERCISE 45

Another possibility could be slurring notes that are farther apart than two adjacent notes in the scale. In this case, E to G, 1st finger to 3rd finger.

EXERCISE 46

And last, before we play our song, the possibility of going from one string to another, all on the same bow stroke. Here, A to G. Open A to G, with the 3rd finger on the D string. Let's try it.

We'll break the song down into exercises first.

EXERCISE 47

EXERCISE 48

EXERCISE 49

EXERCISE 50

GO TELL AUNT RHODY

Play along with the CD or DVD many times until you feel comfortable with slurs.

EXERCISE 51

Here are some more exercises for practicing slurs. Play smoothly and connect the notes.

EXERCISE 52

EXERCISE 53

THE D SCALE

Let's learn two more notes. They'll be C# & D on the A string.

EXERCISE 54

On the staff, C# is found on the next to top space, and the key signature tells us that it's sharp. D is the next to top line. They are noted with the second and third fingers of the left hand respectively. C# is an inch or so above the B with the second finger. D is located just above the C# with the third finger touching or nearly touching the second finger. The distance between notes on the 2nd string follow the same pattern as the distance between notes on the 3rd string. Let's accustom ourselves to these new notes with some answer backs. First A to C#.

EXERCISE 55

EXERCISE 56

Here are some two string answer backs using the open first string or E string. The note sounded by the first string is found on the top space.

34

EXERCISE 57

← Teacher → ← Student →

EXERCISE 58

We now have enough notes to complete a D major scale. Here it is in half notes.

EXERCISE 59

Now we'll play it a little faster, using quarter notes

EXERCISE 60

To build your sense of tonality, also play arpeggios. An arpeggio is a chord, only with the notes sounded one at a time. Our D arpeggio will have D, F#, A, and high D, both ascending and descending.

Do plenty of listening to the CD, because you are training your ears to hear how high or low these notes are as you are training your fingers to find the exact location. In this sense you can't play what you can't hear, so listen carefully and intently.

EXERCISE 61

In Exercises 61 through 64, listen carefully to the distances or intervals between notes.

EXERCISE 64

3/4 TIME

To play the next song, we'll need some new rhythmic concepts. First 3/4 time. If you recall, the top number in the time signature indicates the number of beats per measure, in this case 3. The quarter note receives one beat as shown by the bottom number. 3/4 feels very different than 4/4. Instead of 1,2,3,4, it counts as 123,123. Notes that receive 3 beats are dotted half notes. The principle here is that a dot placed after a note increases its time value by half: in this case 2 beats increases to 3. In written music, rests indicate that you sound no note for a given duration.

EXERCISE 65

Let's practice playing in four bar segments, like this.

EXERCISE 66

Start the bow at the tip.

EXERCISE 67

Start with the bow at the tip and begin with an up bow.

EXERCISE 68

SUNDAY WALTZ

    This concludes the material contained in the *Fiddle DVD*. Make sure you review all of this material and can play it correctly before moving on. Practice along with the DVD or CD until you are comfortable with all the songs and exercises.

SECTION III
FIDDLE TUNES

The material on the following pages is bonus material that is not included on the DVD. The songs and techniques pertain specifically to fiddling and popular Bluegrass standards. Each song is broken down into exercises that should be practiced and perfected before playing the song. Practice the exercises and songs along with the CD to make sure you are playing them correctly.

The following exercises are for *You Are My Sunshine*. Pay close attention to the ties and dotted half notes.

 EXERCISE 69

* Note - A curved line or tie connecting 2 notes indicates combined time values. Play the total combined number of beats in one bow direction (3 beats).

EXERCISE 70

EXERCISE 71

** Note - A dot placed after a note adds to its time value by 1/2. A half note followed by a dot receives 3 beats.

YOU ARE MY SUNSHINE

NEW NOTES ON THE E STRING

The notes we'll play on the E string (1st string) are the open E, F#, G, and A. We'll play the F# first. It's played with the first finger about as far up the string as the E note on the D string (page 26) and the B note on the A string (page 26). It's location on the staff is on the top line.

EXERCISE 72

EXERCISE 73

Here's a two string answer back with a lower open string for reference.

EXERCISE 74

EXERCISE 75

EXERCISE 76

EXERCISE 77

 # WILDWOOD FLOWER

EIGHTH NOTES

In our next tune we'll have a new time value, eighth notes. Two eighth notes equal one quarter note in duration. They are counted 1 & 2 & 3 &. For the eighth note, use about half the distance on the bow as you would for a quarter note. Here are some exercises to prepare you for the eighth notes in *Hot Corn Cold Corn* & *Amazing Grace*.

EXERCISE 78

EXERCISE 82

EXERCISE 83

HOT CORN COLD CORN

EXERCISE 84

EXERCISE 85

EXERCISE 86

AMAZING GRACE

DOTTED RHYTHMS

A dot placed after a note increases it's time value by one half as noted on page 37. A dotted quarter note would then get 1 1/2 counts.

EXERCISE 87

EXERCISE 88

EXERCISE 89

EXERCISE 90

EXERCISE 91

Go to page 50 and play Exercises 96 - 99 to learn the G natural note in the 3rd line.

BLIND MARY

C NATURAL

C natural is played with the 2nd finger on the A string. Place it close to the first finger. Play along with the CD for the following answer backs.

EXERCISE 92

EXERCISE 93

EXERCISE 94

EXERCISE 95

G NATURAL

G natural is found on the space above the top line. It's played with the second finger close to the F# note.

EXERCISE 96

EXERCISE 97

EXERCISE 98

EXERCISE 99

EXERCISE 100

EXERCISE 101

EXERCISE 102

STAR OF THE COUNTY DOWN

EXERCISE 103

EXERCISE 104

EXERCISE 105

SOUTHWIND

EXERCISE 106

EXERCISE 107

EXERCISE 108

WILL THE CIRCLE BE UNBROKEN

THE A NOTE

The A note is located on the first ledger line above the staff. It is played with the 3rd finger.

EXERCISE 109

EXERCISE 110

EXERCISE 111

EXERCISE 112

Here are the first five notes of the D major scale played an octave higher.

EXERCISE 113

EXERCISE 114

EXERCISE 115

ANGELINE THE BAKER

EXERCISE 116

EXERCISE 117

EXERCISE 118

LITTLE MAGGIE

DOUBLE STOPS

A double stop occurs when you play two strings on the fiddle at the same time. Practice the following exercises to do double stops.

EXERCISE 119

EXERCISE 120

EXERCISE 121

EXERCISE 122

SHUFFLE

The Georgia Shuffle is the most common bowing pattern in fiddle music. It can be played on one or two strings, with any left hand fingering. Note that the long note in every other group is a down bow and every other alternating note is an up bow. Practice the following exercises.

EXERCISE 123

EXERCISE 124

Here are two exercises that combine the shuffle with double stops.

EXERCISES 125

EXERCISES 126

We'll combine the Georgia Shuffle bowing pattern and double stops in this next tune.

BOIL THEM CABBAGE DOWN

Make sure you practice along with the CD to get the proper feel for the shuffle.

EXERCISE 128

SOLDIER'S JOY

Note - Starting with *Soldier's Joy*, we will not play the repeats on the CD because of time constraints. However, make sure you always practice the repeats and get in the habit of playing them because that's how other musicians will be playing the songs.

EXERCISE 129

EXERCISE 130

EXERCISE 131

CRIPPLE CREEK

EXERCISE 132

EXERCISE 133

EXERCISE 134

RED HAIRED BOY

EXERCISE 135

EXERCISE 136

EXERCISE 137

SALT CREEK

EXERCISE 138

EXERCISE 139

EXERCISE 140

ROLL IN MY SWEET BABY'S ARMS

OLD JOE CLARK

Notes